ALEXANDRA WEMER

ROOTED *in* RIGHTEOUSNESS

31 Devotions to Grow Your Faith
& Renew Your Mind

"Therefore, as you received Christ Jesus the Lord, so walk in Him, rooted and built up in Him and established in the faith, just as you were taught, abounding in thanksgiving."

Colossians 2:6-7 ESV

To my husband,

Thank you for supporting all of my endeavors and loving me as Christ loved the church.
I love you and our story.

TABLE OF CONTENTS

INTRODUCTION

Hey, sister! I am so grateful you picked up this book. Whether you are taking your first step into a deeper relationship with God or continuing your ongoing faith journey, I pray this devotional becomes a place where your heart feels seen, your soul finds rest, and your faith grows stronger.

As women, God has uniquely designed each of us. We often serve as nurturers, homemakers, and sources of warmth and light to those around us. Yet, in the midst of our many roles, it's vital to remember who we are in Christ. No matter where you find yourself—whether at the peak of a mountain or in the depths of a valley—you are seen, loved, and chosen by Him. You are qualified by God and He has special purpose for your life. His promise to you remains steadfast: "For I know the plans I have for you," declares the Lord, "plans for welfare and not for evil, to give you a future and a hope" (Jeremiah 29:11).

I am excited to spend the next thirty-one days in God's Word with you. I encourage you to dive deeply into the referenced scriptures throughout each day, meditate on them, and write them on the tablet of your heart. His Word renews our minds, keeps us in perfect peace, and breathes life and healing into our body (Proverbs 4:22).

My prayer is that this devotional opens the eyes of your heart and stirs your spirit, providing you with fresh revelation of God's love and truth. I pray it deepens your relationship with the Father, igniting a fire within your spirit to run after Him wholeheartedly. By the end of this journey, I believe you'll see Jesus reflected in your life as you allow Him to refine and purify you.

This devotional was written with *you* in mind—the woman longing to deepen her roots in Christ while navigating the beauty and challenges of life. You are here reading this book because of Jesus, not by any coincidence.

So, what are you waiting for? Let's get started!

With love,

Alexandra

MADE NEW
DAY 1

Galatians 2:20
2 Corinthians 5:17-21

When we give our lives to Jesus and accept Him into our hearts, the Bible tells us that we become a new creation in Christ. The old self has died, and now Christ lives in us. We are spiritually united with the Lord, and our identity is shaped not by our past sins or worldly standards, but by the sacrifice Jesus made on the cross and His resurrection. Sin no longer separates us from the Lord; our former way of life is gone, and our new self emerges. This new self is holy, pure, and righteous in the eyes of Christ.

Being a new creation involves more than a superficial change; it is a deep transformation of our heart, mind, and soul. Jesus's death on the cross completely eradicated our sins, and we are forgiven and redeemed—our sins no longer exist. Thank you, Jesus! When we repent, He casts all our sins into a sea of forgetfulness. Stop revisiting your past with God. The enemy (the devil) seeks to remind you of your hurts to distract you and prevent you from receiving and walking in what God desires for you.

As we undergo this transformation, our heart begin to soften. The Holy Spirit works within us, helping us resemble Jesus more closely when we fully surrender our lives to Him. Jesus removes our desire to sin as we did in the past, and the things we used to partake in no longer appeal to us. In exchange for our burdens, He gives us joy and supernatural peace. When we ask, He uproots the things within us that do not belong. This is the sanctification process—the journey of becoming more like Christ. This new life in Christ includes the promise and hope of eternal life spent with God in heaven forever.

In Colossians 3:1-4, scripture instructs us to put on the new self. Later in verse 3:13, we are commanded to forgive others. This is a powerful reminder. The new self embodies discipline and does not hold grudges. Let us strive to forgive like Jesus, embracing our identity as a new creation in Him. In this scripture, forgiveness is not presented as an option, but as a command. This allows the peace of Christ to rule in our hearts (Colossians 3:15). Through Jesus, we are not merely improved but completely renewed in His great and perfect love as our identity aligns with God's purpose for us.

Reflect:

As a new creation in Christ, how can I better reflect Jesus today? Who do I need to genuinely forgive?

Pray:

Lord, help me to set aside my old ways and anything that does not align with Your heart. Give me the strength to surrender my pride, selfishness, and any habits that hinder me from fully living in Your truth. May my actions, words, and thoughts be shaped by Your example, enabling me to love others with the same compassion and grace that You show to me. As I learn from Your Word, I pray it transforms me from the inside out, allowing Your goodness to shine through to those around me. In Jesus' name, Amen.

DEPENDING ON GOD
DAY 2

Isaiah 41:10
Philippians 4:13
John 15:5

If you were anything like me, you may have grown up striving for self-sufficiency and independence, often refraining from asking for help due to feeling like a burden to others. However, this mindset has led me down many dead ends and broken roads. I quickly realized I couldn't accomplish anything meaningful, nor would I want to, without God's presence in my life. After I accepted Jesus into my heart, I learned that God delights in our requests for help. He desires to provide and care for us. We were not created to be self-sufficient because we need the help of our Savior. John 15:5 says, "He is the true vine, we are the branches". Here we are reminded God is the sole giver of life. All good things are from the Father, including our gifts and talents. He is the one who produces good fruit in us and apart from Him, we can do nothing.

His plan for us is always greater than the one we have outlined for ourselves. We desperately need His unconditional love, wisdom, and strength to guide us. When we walk with Him, He protects us from paths filled with pain, heartache, and disappointment. Often, our greatest worries reveal the areas in which we trust God the least. I encourage you today to fix your eyes on Jesus instead of your circumstances and give it to God. In the Bible, it says God left nothing out of His control (Hebrews 2:8). If He said it, He meant it.

As you draw near to God, He draws nearer to you, filling you with peace. When our security rests solely in God, our true provider, peace that surpasses all understanding will follow. We can do all things with Christ because we serve a God who can accomplish what looks to be impossible.

Reflect:

What do you need to give to God today to find peace?

Pray:

Thank you, Lord, for leading me and guiding me into all truth. Thank you that whenever I need wisdom, I only have to ask for it. Thank you for your provision and protection and for never leaving or forsaking me. Thank you for Your promises, Your Word that guides me, and Your presence that brings me peace. Lord, teach me to lean on You more each day, to trust in Your goodness, and to rest in the assurance of Your love. In Jesus' name, Amen.

WHO GOD SAYS I AM
DAY 3

1 Peter 2:9
Romans 8:35-39
Deuteronomy 28:13

The world today is struggling with an identity crisis, but as believers, we are called to stand firm in who we are because God's Word clearly defines us. You have authority over your mind—it's not up to the enemy to control your thoughts! With the Holy Spirit living within us, we carry God's peace and joy in our hearts. Today's scripture says we are chosen, a royal priesthood, a holy nation, and God's special possession. It also states that we are more than conquerors through Him who loved us. How reassuring it is to know that nothing can separate us from Christ's love.

These scriptures are powerful truths. This is exactly how God describes His people. They serve as wonderful daily reminders that we are loved and cherished by God beyond measure. When doubt arises or you begin to think negatively about yourself, I pray you quickly refer to these scriptures. You are a child of God! Let God's Word remind you of your worth each day of your life.

You were created for a time such as this (Esther 4:14). God has placed us exactly where we are at this very moment because He has a purpose and plan for our lives. Don't let the voice of the enemy tell you any different. We are loved and chosen. We are seated in heavenly places with Christ. If Christ has no rival, we also have no rival! Stop believing that you are worthless. Stop believing that you will never get married, or that you have failed your children. Stop believing that you are stuck where you are. These are lies from the enemy! You are redeemed and forgiven. He has a plan to prosper you! As you'll read tomorrow, the more we meditate on God's Word, the better equipped we are for the battle of our minds.

In John 15:15, Jesus says, "I no longer call you servants...Instead, I have called you friends." We're invited into a close, personal relationship with God, sharing in His love and heart. What a friend we have in Jesus! Each of these identities point back to God's love and grace toward us, reassuring us of our value and purpose in Him. Through Christ, our identity is secure, unchanging, and filled with unshakable purpose.

Reflect:

What do you believe about yourself? Does this align with the Word of God?

Pray:

Jesus, I am deeply grateful that You see me as Your child—chosen, redeemed, and cherished by You. Thank You for making me a new creation in Christ, forgiven and set free from my past. I thank You for the new life and purpose You have given me. Help me walk boldly in my identity as Your ambassador, sharing Your love and grace with the world around me today. In Jesus' name, Amen.

WALKING IN VICTORY
DAY 4

1 Corinthians 15: 55-57
Luke 10:19

I have been in conversations before with Christians who say things like, "I hope we can make it through this" or "I hope God comes through for us". All I want to ask is, where is your faith?

As children of the highest King, we do not need to ask God for the victory, because we already possess it. When God died upon the cross, He defeated every principality of darkness and stole the key to hell and the grave. He conquered death and gave us authority. In today's scriptures, we read that Jesus gave us authority over all the power of the enemy, and nothing shall hurt us.

Through His precious blood, we have achieved victory over Satan and death. In the spiritual realm, Jesus' blood not only signifies a new covenant and atonement for sin, but also grants us access to God's presence, freedom, and power. Revelation 12:11 tells us,

"They triumphed over him by the blood of the Lamb and by the word of their testimony." Jesus' blood symbolizes the enemy's defeat, breaking the power of sin, death, and any bondage that once held us captive.

Every battle you face today has already been won by the blood of Jesus Christ, no matter what it might look like in the natural realm. God fights for us against our enemies to grant us victory (Deuteronomy 20:4). Because of His favor, any enemy that rises against us will be defeated in the name of Jesus! No battle is too great for the God we serve. Though our enemies may come against us one way, they will scatter in seven (Deuteronomy 28:7).

When I think about holding the victory, I am reminded of David's battle with Goliath. David approached the giant from a position of victory, though armed with only a few stones. He spoke to Goliath with God-given confidence, knowing that God would never fail him. Be confident that God will fight for you, no matter how daunting the battle may seem. We will not be overtaken or overcome by our enemies.

Reflect:

What battle or trial are you facing today that you need to surrender to God?

Prayer:

Thank you, Jesus, for shedding your precious blood on the cross for me as the perfect sacrifice. Thank you, Jesus, that I fight from a position of victory and no enemy can ever defeat me. Thank you, Lord, for forgiveness and redemption. Thank you for the power and authority you have given me through Your blood. In Jesus' name, Amen.

DISCOVERING OUR PURPOSE
DAY 5

Proverbs 3:5-6
Psalm 37:4
Ephesians 2:10

Have you ever pondered over your purpose? In a world that associates purpose with achievement, education, wealth, and success, it's easy to feel pressured to define ourselves by our careers or financial status. However, God qualifies us, not man. In Christ, our purpose has a greater meaning—it is deeply personal, uniquely crafted, and rooted in the Lord. God has created us with a specific purpose; a calling that reflects His love and glory.

Ephesians 2:10 tells us that we are "God's handiwork," meaning we are crafted by His hands. Each of us are thoughtfully designed with strengths, gifts, and talents that each serve a kingdom purpose. God created us with intention. He made no mistakes. You are fearfully and wonderfully made by God (Psalm 139:14).

Discovering our purpose begins by understanding our identity in Christ. Instead of looking outward to define who we are, we look to the Word of God. When we root our identity in Christ, our lives gain meaning. Then our true desires align with God's purpose and plan for our lives, whether that involves being a wife, a mother, starting a podcast, or writing a book. As we learn to delight ourselves in the Lord, He fulfills the desires of our hearts in accordance with His will. With God, we have everything we will ever need. Proverbs 3 reminds us not to lean on our own understanding but to trust that the Lord has our best interests in mind. If God is for us, who can be against us (Romans 8:31)?

Reflect:

What gifts and talents has the Lord given you? How can these gifts reflect His purpose for you and guide you in your actions?

Pray:

Lord, thank You for creating me with purpose. Help me to find my identity in You, knowing that I am Your masterpiece. Open the eyes of my heart to understand the unique calling You have placed upon my life. Reveal Your purpose to me and help me trust that You are guiding me every step of the way. May my life be a testament to Your grace and purpose, bringing You glory. In Jesus' name, Amen.

GOD'S PLAN
DAY 6

Isaiah 58:11
Proverbs 20:24
Philippians 4:6-7

I remember sitting in my bedroom around 15 years old, trying to plan each major milestone of my life. I would graduate college at 21, get married at 23, and start having children by 25. I quickly realized, no matter how hard I tried to devise my own plans for the future, it is the Lord who establishes my steps (Proverbs 16:9). As we read today, His purpose will prevail. And let me tell you, God is really good at exceeding expectations. For that, I am extremely thankful.

The assignment God calls us to carry out sometimes doesn't make sense in the natural and often comes with great opposition from the people who are near to us. To many, it might seem like the wrong decision; to others, it might appear impossible. I would rather follow the leading of the Holy Spirit and step out in faith with boldness than try to do anything on my own with limited understanding. His thoughts are higher than our thoughts, and His ways are higher than our ways (Isaiah 55:9). We are commanded not to be anxious about anything!

Job 42:2 says, "I know that you can do all things; no purpose of yours can be thwarted." When an opportunity is from God, it will come with peace and confirmation. Being led by the Spirit means we are sensitive to hearing His whisper and discerning His guidance. There are things the Bible doesn't tell us to do—such as what state to move to or which job offer to accept—but when we become sensitive, seeking the Lord in all we do, we can begin to know God's plan for us. He will reveal new things to us and give us wisdom when we ask (James 1:5). I once heard someone say, "God doesn't lay out the whole blueprint for your life because if He did, faith wouldn't be necessary. Trusting God wouldn't be as crucial." Stepping out in faith is needed to obey His direction. Remember, faith without works is dead! (James 2:17) Faith is an action word, and often causes us to step out of our comfort zone.

Reflect:

In what area of your life do you need direction from the Holy Spirit? Where is the Lord asking you to step out in faith today?

Pray:

Thank You, Lord, for being my strong tower and for continuing to guide and direct my path. Thank You for the plans You have for my life—plans filled with hope, purpose, and promise. Even when I may not understand the path before me, I trust that Your ways are higher and that You are working everything for my good. I submit to Your plans because I am confident they are better than my own. In Jesus' name, Amen.

THE PICTURE OF PRAISE
DAY 7

Psalm 150

What does praise look like to you? Is it the sounds of birds chirping or squirrels chattering to one another? Is it singing worship songs at church on Sunday mornings? Is it softly muttering "Thank you, God" in mundane moments? I believe praise encompasses all these things. These scriptures encourage us to praise the Lord in every moment, regardless of our circumstances, because He alone is worthy. At night, we should go to bed praising the Lord, thanking Him for the day and every opportunity. We should wake up each morning and praise the Lord, thanking Him for another day and the breath in our lungs. By starting our day with praise, we can shape the direction and outcome of the day.

Jesus inhabits the praises of His people (Psalm 22:3). Praise is the quickest way to enter God's presence. When we lift our voices in praise, we activate His wonder-working power in our lives. Entering His presence with thanksgiving strengthens us and gives us peace. I can't make it through a day without entering His presence. It transforms my reactions, my words, and my ability to handle difficult situations so I can respond with gentleness and love.

At times, we might praise on behalf of our families, friends, or even our bosses, knowing that mighty things can happen. God can do all things, including those that seem impossible. When I was younger, I used to watch people in church raising their hands and jumping around, and I didn't have a clue what they were doing or why they were doing it. Now, I am one of those people. I praise God for who He is and for everything He has brought me through (and I will dance and jump around about it). We may not know what others are praising God for; they might be praising for God for a breakthrough or a miracle. Today, even if you don't feel like it, praise Him. Satan isn't scared of a silent Christian; he wants to keep your mouth closed. When you don't open your mouth to pray or praise, you lose by default. Your silence won't provoke God to move, and it surely won't move that mountain in your way. Our words are weapons in the spirit.

Praise provokes the move of God and draws Him near to us (Mark 10:46-52). One example in scripture is when Bartimaeus was praising Jesus by confirming that He is who he says he is. Bartimaeus's praise was an outward display of faith. Without faith, it is impossible to please God (Hebrews 11:6). We can praise God in faith by thanking Him for what He is about to do and setting our expectations upon Him. When we spend time with the Lord in our secret place, we should expect to leave changed each time—with a word from Him or with new revelation knowledge, and always with peace. We praise Him first and foremost for who He is, but also for everything He has done for us and everything He is about to do!

Reflect:

Make a list of twenty things you are thankful for, then thank God for each one. Develop the habit of thanking God first in your prayer time.

Pray:

Thank you, Jesus, for direct access to you. I am so grateful to serve a God who cares for His children deeply with great compassion. Help me clearly see all the things I have to be thankful for during this season. Thank you for every blessing you have given me. I pour out my praise to you today. You are worthy of all honor and glory. In Jesus' name, Amen.

YOUR CONFESSION
DAY 8

Proverbs 18:21
Mark 11:22-25

The Bible says the tongue is a small part of the body, yet it boasts of great things (James 3:5). Many people do not understand the significant power our words hold. With our words, we can build up others; with our words, we can also tear them down. Our words can bring life or destruction to a situation. Seed time and harvest is a spiritual law that also applies to our words. For example, if you plant carrot seeds, you expect carrots to grow where you planted the seeds. In other words, you reap what you sow (Galatians 6:7). The same is true with the words we speak. If you plant seeds of complaints and negativity, you'll reap situations that do not go your way. Like I mentioned yesterday, our words are weapons in the spirit. With our words, we can rebuke the devourer. Fight your battles by immersing yourself in the Word of God.

Scripture reminds us in 2 Timothy 3:16, "All scripture is breathed out by God and profitable for teaching, for reproof, for correction, and for training in righteousness". I'm sure that confessing scripture over your life will enable you to walk in supernatural strength when you speak the same words Jesus spoke.

Moreover, the Bible also teaches us that life and death are in the power of the tongue. Our tongue can lead us down a path of blessings or destruction. Even complaining plants seeds of destruction. Consider the things you might not enjoy and are quick to complain about. Now, try reframing those thoughts and confessing "I get to" statements. I get to go to work today. I get to raise a family. I get to make money to support my family. What a blessing.

We are to continually put on the garment of praise each day for all God has given us and for all He will provide. When our heart remains in a posture of gratitude, we don't have any time to ponder on the things we wish we had or compare our lives to others around us. Gratitude is a weapon we use against the enemy who wants to keep us depressed and oppressed. We are called to give thanks in all circumstances, as this is Christ's will for us (1 Thessalonians 5:16-18). Faith is released by speaking (2 Corinthians 4:13). What will you choose to speak this week? I encourage you to be more mindful of your words throughout each day.

Reflect:

What have you been speaking recently? Will your words bring life or destruction this week?

Pray:

Lord, help me to be more attentive to the words I speak. Teach me to recognize the weight of my words. Teach me to be slow to anger and slow to speak. Guard my tongue from negativity and complaints that do not reflect Your heart. Instead, fill my mouth with grace, kindness, and wisdom, so that I may lift up those around me and bring glory to Your name. In Jesus' name, Amen.

PATIENCE IN THE WAITING
DAY 9

Romans 8:25
Galatians 6:9
Romans 12:12

I'm convinced everyone loves the word patience. It is just so simple to walk in, isn't it? False. In today's world, we have access to everything at our fingertips. We live in a world of the now. If I buy something from Amazon, I can have it in 3-4 hours. On other sites, we can even pay for expedited shipping to have our order the next business day. We live in a world that neglects patience.

Patience is something we must exercise daily. The Lord tells us in these scriptures that we must be patient to receive the promises of God. If God sees the beginning and the end; in fact, He is the beginning and the end, then we must be confident He has it all worked out for us. Romans 8:35 reads, "But if we hope for what we do not yet have, we wait for it patiently." Easier said than done, right?

God sees beyond our human limitations. He sees not only who we are now, but who He created us to be. For this reason, He will never give up on us. As Pastor Samuel Fitch once said, "Don't allow your carnal mind to impose limits on a supernatural God". He often exceeds our expectations by the power working within us (Ephesians 3:20), but we first must have an expectation of what God will do.

Part of God's blessing lies in the transformation that occurs during the waiting. In our waiting, God is refining us and teaching us new things. Preparation time is never wasted time. He is preparing us for what we are waiting for. Walk confidently in faith, not by sight, because we can trust that God will fulfill His promises. Scripture assures us, "I am watching over my word to perform it" (Jeremiah 1:12).

In Hebrews 6, it states that Abraham waited patiently to obtain God's promises. Key word: patiently. We know Abraham eventually obtained the God's promises and was named "The Father of many nations." Abraham and his wife waited twenty-five years for a son. God always has a purpose in the waiting; therefore, remain steadfast and anchored in hope.

For encouragement, read Hebrews Chapter 11. It describes many people throughout scripture who exhibited unwavering faith. What an example they set! Each of these individuals must have endured hardships, and in every circumstance, their faith was tested. Yet they remained obedient and trusted God.

Faith involves trusting God, while patience means continuing to trust Him, even when it's tough. Do not waver in your faith or attempt to help God fulfill His promise. If you find yourself in a waiting season, I hope this message encourages you. God is never late. As 2 Peter 3:9 states, God is not slow to fulfill His promise. If He has placed a word in your spirit, you can be confident it will come to pass. He is always right on time (Isaiah 60:22).

Reflect:

Are you in a waiting season? If so, how can you draw nearer to God today and grow your faith?

Pray:

Thank you, Jesus, for being with me in every season. Give me patience and help me trust in Your perfect timing. Teach me to lean on You and to seek You during this time. May this season of waiting strengthen my relationship with You and prepare me for all You have for me in the future. In Jesus' name, Amen.

CALL UNTO HIM
DAY 10

Psalm 46:10
Matthew 7:7

Yesterday we found peace in understanding that God is orchestrating everything for our good and will bring it to fruition at the proper time. In this time of waiting, we have the chance to draw closer to God each day. This includes immersing ourselves in His Word, as it holds many hidden truths that we can only discover through reading. God knows our needs before we even ask. Scripture reminds us that we have not because we ask not (James 4:2-3). We are told to ask, and it will be given to you, seek, and you will find, knock, and it will be opened to you.

When we ask God for something and expect Him to respond, our faith grows. Jeremiah 33:3 reads, "Call to me and I will answer you, and will tell you great and hidden things that you have not known." It is essential that we remain sensitive and responsive to

His whisper during our waiting. If you have yet to hear the voice of the Lord, you need to spend more time in fellowship with Him. Afterall, the more time you spend with someone the more clearly you recognize their voice.

A great way to start praying in your waiting is to thank God for the thing you are waiting for as if you already have it. This is a declaration of your faith. If you are waiting for something, thank God that it is YOURS! This invites God's action on your behalf, as He delights in giving good gifts and blessings to His children.

Take a moment to pause and recognize that God is with you in every moment, even when you don't feel or see Him working on your behalf. He is always arranging things for your good and will meet every need you bring to Him. He takes away burdens and replaces them with peace. Often in prayer, we don't stop talking or asking. Prayer is not a one-way street.

God speaks to us in different ways. For some it may be dreams and visions, for some it may be through His Word, for some He may use others around us to speak to us. As I have grown closer to the Lord, I have recognized the importance of silence in prayer. How can you hear from the Lord if you cannot be still or spend the entirety of your prayer time doing all the talking? Take time to be silent, wait, and listen for the Lord today in your prayer time. When we are quiet and our hearts are open and ready to receive, the Lord will show up at the right time with the right word to reach our heart.

Reflect:

How can you draw nearer to God this week?

Pray:

Lord, thank you for Your presence. Please quiet the noise around me and release the distractions and anxieties in my mind so I may hear Your voice clearly. I want to rest in Your presence, knowing that You comfort me and lead me in love. Grant me sensitivity and responsiveness to hear Your whisper better than ever before. Direct my path and be the lamp unto my feet today. In Jesus' name, I pray, Amen.

OUR GREAT SHEPHERD
DAY 11

Luke 15:11-32
John 10:11, 27-29

Today we read Jesus refers to Himself as the Good Shepherd. A shepherd is defined as someone who directs and guides, tending to the safety of others. No matter how far we run or have run from the Lord, He will continue to fight for us. If one of His sheep goes astray, the Bible tells us he leaves the ninety-nine for the one. God will never give up on His children, so when we return to the Lord, He welcomes us with arms wide open, just as this father did in the parable of the lost son. Not only does He welcome His children home, but when He finds the lost sheep, "he joyfully puts it on his shoulders and goes home" (Luke 15:5). That's what Jesus does!

Looking back on my life, I can admit to times I have fallen away from the things of God. Never in my past did I see myself serving

God in a church where I am now a leader. I never imagined talking to people I barely know about the great things God has done for me and taking the initiative to pray for others in mid-conversation. I had never envisioned myself leading others in worship on a platform, but behold, God has a plan. I can do all things through Christ who strengthens me (Philippians 4:13). He changes everything.

As humans, we can only see our past and our present, but God sees our future. He sees us for who He has created us to be. He sees our kingdom purpose, which He will help us accomplish. He has already equipped us with everything we need. You were created for a time such as this. God will use you to accomplish His purpose. I pray you surrender yourself to God's will and ask Him to use you, but only if you mean it. He will transform your life if you let Him.

Reflect:

Think back on your life. When has Jesus left the ninety-nine to find and rescue you? Thank Him for never giving up on you.

Pray:

Lord, thank You for leading me beside still waters and restoring my soul when I am weary. In You, I find comfort, peace, and guidance, knowing that I am safe in Your loving care. Lord, remind me daily that You are near, that I am never alone, and that You can make a way where there seems to be no way. Help me to follow Your voice, to trust in Your wisdom, and to rest in Your care. In Jesus' name, Amen.

TASTE AND SEE
DAY 12

Psalm 34

Today's psalm represents thanksgiving and trust in the Lord. These scriptures serve as a beautiful reminder of God's faithfulness, protection, and goodness toward those who seek Him. David, the author of this psalm, wrote these verses of praise after God delivered him from many trials throughout his life. The more we seek Christ, the more we will find Him as He becomes our hiding place, our refuge, and our strong tower.

David understood what it meant to face the fear of the unknown, yet he chose to continue praising God regardless of his circumstances. In moments of hardship and adversity, we are called to praise God. In moments of joy and restoration, we are called to praise God. This is because He is good, and His mercies endure forever. David's invitation to taste and see that the Lord is good is deeply personal. Each of us has experienced God's goodness in different and wonderful ways. His perfect love never fails those who take refuge in Him. God is always ready to be the guiding light to our path leading us into the comforting embrace of His love.

We cannot interpret God's character by our circumstances. God is good, even when our circumstances are not because that is His very nature. He never changes. We can be confident that even when situations around us look to be crashing and burning, God is working. He has our best interests in mind. Spend time in prayer today, thanking God for His goodness, and reflect on how He has been faithful in your life. Ask Him to help you deepen your revelation of His goodness today.

Reflect:

How have you tasted and seen that the Lord has been good in your life?

Pray:

Lord, I come before You with a heart full of gratitude. Thank You for perfect love, for Your goodness and for Your mercies that are new every morning. I am grateful for every blessing, both big and small, seen and unseen. Strengthen my heart, Lord, so that I may face each day with confidence in Your goodness. In Jesus' name, Amen.

FIGHTING TEMPTATIONS
DAY 13

Luke 4:1-13
1 Corinthians 10:13

I can think back to many times where the Lord convicted me of the sin I was living in and pulled me out. Jesus loves us too much to let us remain where we are. In today's scriptures, we read Jesus was also tempted and tried, but did not sin once. To fight and withstand temptations, Jesus declared, "It is written." This declaration carried more authority than both the tempter and the temptation itself. This is exactly what we need to do when we are tempted by the enemy to fall into sin. In James 1:13, we read that God does not tempt anyone. As a matter of fact, Hebrews 2:18 reads that God can help those being tempted.

The more we read the Bible and meditate on scripture, the more equipped we become to withstand the lies and schemes of the enemy. He has no new tricks! He wants to drag us off course and destroy us. He wants to steal our thoughts and everything good God has given us. But we must put on the mind of Christ every day. We need to put on the armor of God, as described in Ephesians 6:10-18. The Bible is our sword of the spirit. Hebrews states that the Word is living and active, sharper than a double-edged sword. There is no greater weapon God could give us. In Hebrews 4:15-16, we learn that because Jesus was tempted and tried, He can sympathize with us in our weakness. God understands the sting of rejection too. When we are weak, we must ask for strength, and God will help us move away from temptations.

The coming of the Lord is near, so now more than ever we need to run from sin in the opposite direction. With God's help, the wicked things we once desired won't appeal to us anymore. God is merciful and changes our hearts to remove desires that are not from Him and do not give Him glory. Ask the Lord for strength and grace to stand firm against sin and temptation. Jesus will provide a way out of temptations every time.

Reflect:

What temptations have you been giving into recently? How can you prevent yourself from succumbing to these temptations next time? Write down three scriptures you can recite to help give you strength in moments of weakness.

Pray:

Lord, I thank You for providing a way out of every temptation. Fill me with Your Spirit so that I may stand firm and resist temptations. Replace my weaknesses with Your strength, my doubts with Your truth, and my desires with a deeper love for You. Help me to seek Your will above all else and to trust that You are all that I need. Remind me that in every struggle, You are with me, and You are faithful. In Jesus' name, Amen.

THE INVITATION TO REST
DAY 14

Matthew 11:28-30
Matthew 8:23-27

Our days can be exhausting. I sometimes find myself dragging myself out the door to work or to previous events I said "yes" to but then have little motivation to attend later. Every day, I am so thankful that Jesus is my strength. If you are a people pleaser (or used to be), this one is for you. I came to the realization quickly that one goal on earth is to please and honor Jesus, not anyone else. What I'm getting at is that you don't have to say yes to everyone or everything when people ask. You must consider the state of your soul. We are called to live with a sincere heart, fearing the Lord, not as people pleasers (Colossians 3:22).

The enemy likes to keep us busy in our daily lives. He knows that when we are busy, we are distracted. He wants us too distracted to get into the presence of God and sit at His feet. Satan wants you too distracted to pray and read your Bible. Thankfully, in Matthew 11:28, Jesus says, "Come to me, all of you who are weary and burdened, and I will give you rest." God wants your best. God wants you to be effective for His kingdom. It's hard to do that when we are running on empty trying to provide for our families working three or more jobs. Many fill their schedules to the brim and wonder why they feel so far from Jesus. Have you spent time with Him today without distractions?

Here's some advice for you: Be intentional about spending time with God. I always set aside an hour in the morning to pray and spend time in the Word. It refreshes and restores my soul for the day ahead, even if it means waking up an hour earlier than usual. I promise you, it is worth it. Create a plan this week to spend uninterrupted time with Jesus. God wants us to live in a peace that surpasses all understanding. In the scriptures today, we see that Jesus was so filled with peace that He was able to sleep in the middle of the storm. When it feels like the waves are overtaking us, we are called to find rest in Jesus. There is nothing like the presence of the Lord.

Recently I saw an Instagram post that said, "Overworking yourself is not an achievement". This is spot on. Overworking yourself will lead to burnout, and burnout to discontentment and feelings of sorrow. When you are burnt out from your job or career, what is left for you to give Jesus? I'm not letting anyone, or anything steal my peace and joy. The world can't take it away. Peace and joy are my birthright in Jesus' name. I encourage you today to think about the things that are not benefiting you and are just taking up too much of your time. Ask God to reveal any distractions in your life that are no longer serving you. In Genesis, remember that even God rested on the seventh day after He created all things. We are called to rest.

Reflect:

What is God leading you to say "no" to this week? What is He nudging you to make more time for?

Pray:

Lord, I come to You today in need of rest. Help me lay down all that troubles and burdens. Teach me to release my anxieties and trust that You are in full control. Let my heart find rest in You alone, knowing that You are faithful and that Your grace is enough. Help me prioritize spending time in Your presence each day. Thank You for lifting every burden and replacing my overwhelming feelings with peace. In Jesus' name, Amen.

WORKING FOR THE LORD
DAY 15

Colossians 3:23-24

Today we read about serving the Lord in all we do. There have been moments in my life when I hesitated to go the extra mile at my job because nobody else was, and I knew my efforts wouldn't be acknowledged. Maybe you have experienced this too. But in this scripture, Paul reminds us that our reward is not here on earth, but rather our inheritance through Christ.

Paul also instructs us to work heartily for the Lord, not for men. At your job, it is helpful to imagine God as your boss. This perspective might change your work ethic and how much you care about your responsibilities. When you work for the Lord, you are less likely to cut corners and more likely to pay attention to all aspects of your job, even the tedious details. Remember, you are serving the

Lord, and He sees everything. Scripture tells us to do everything in the name of the Lord to glorify God (1 Corinthians 10:31).

We will be rewarded for our hard work. God sees our efforts, even when it feels like nobody else does. Going the extra mile truly honors God. We are called to honor Him in everything we do and everything we are. Ask God to refocus your mind on honoring Him today. Ask Him to guide your actions and words to honor Him in greater measure today, and then see how much joy fills your heart from serving others for Jesus. Do everything for others without expecting anything in return. Our inheritance is unperishable and unfading in heaven (1 Peter 1:4).

When it comes to serving others, one of the best things I ever did for my marriage was stop keeping score. It's not about counting who did more for the other person that day. It's about loving as Christ loves us—with humility—and doing everything for the Lord. It's about asking God for a heart to serve others, which will blossom into a servant's heart. After all, God doesn't keep score either. Every action, every thoughtful word, and every moment spent helping someone in need becomes a form of worship to God. Our service is not a mere obligation, but an opportunity for us to honor Him.

Reflect:

Who is your heart moved to serve? It could be a group of people or an area of need in your church. Who is on your heart to serve today?

Pray:

Lord, I thank you today for every gift and talent you have given me. Help me to see the needs of those around me and to respond with a willing heart, even in the workplace. May I be quick to serve, slow to judge, and always eager to give more than what is expected. When my flesh wants to cut corners, remind me that I am serving you and that each small act of service has value in Your eyes. Let my actions reflect Your love, and may my heart grow more compassionate each day. In Jesus' name, Amen.

OUR OBEDIENCE IN SURRENDER
DAY 16

Luke 5:4-7
Mark 1:16-18

In today's scriptures, we read that the disciples immediately obeyed Jesus. And they were greatly blessed when they did! We are called to walk away from our selfish interests and greed to follow the Lord, not to conform to the patterns of this world. We are called to be set apart. Jesus is encouraging you to lay down anything getting in the way of Him, because He is worthy. He convicts our hearts, so we know when we are making a wrong choice or going against the Word of God. If there is something He is wanting you to lay down at His feet, you'll know it. Because Jesus sacrificed His life for us, we are to be a living sacrifice for Him (Romans 21:1).

When God removes something from your life, trust that He has something better ahead for you. My mind quickly jumps to the image of Jesus and a little girl standing face to face. She is holding a small teddy bear she loves. Jesus is asking her to give it to Him. Like us in moments of hesitation, she doesn't see the bigger and better teddy bear Jesus is holding behind His back. God never removes something from your life without planning to bless you with something greater.

When God asks you to move or leave your job, people might not understand why. It may not seem logical to the natural mind, but obeying God provokes His favor. We see this when Simon Peter was instructed to cast his net into deep water after they caught nothing all night. Though it didn't make sense, Simon obeyed anyway. As a result of his obedience, he caught so many fish that his net began to break, and both boats started to sink. Not one, but both!

God will never guide you into something that leads to your destruction or is a waste of your time. His power within you will allow you to accomplish whatever He has called you to do. Likewise, God won't anoint you and then leave you to figure things out on your own. He equips us with all we need to carry out the assignments He gives us. Remember that God is always with you; He will never leave you nor forsake you along the way. What God has started, no man can stop!

I encourage you today to stop and look at the bigger picture: we were created by God for God, to witness to others and bring glory to His name. After all, His Word tells us He will return on the clouds with great power and glory. It is important to remember that heaven and earth will pass away, but His word will never pass away (Mark 13:31).

One of my favorite things about surrender is that God fully takes hold of our hearts. In 1 John 3:9-10, we see that God removes sin from us through conviction. He will continue to refine and purify a heart that seeks Him and is surrendered to Him so that we can look more like Jesus in all we do and all we speak. My goal is that others may see Christ shine through me.

Reflect:

What is God asking you to lay down today? Think about any convictions God has brought to your attention recently.

Pray:

Lord, You are holy and righteous. I ask You to reveal the things in me that are not of You. Convict my heart to let go of my selfish desires and any habits that are not pleasing to You. Forgive me for my sins and give me a fresh fire to pursue You today. In Jesus' name, Amen.

CONFIDENCE IN CHRIST
DAY 17

Romans 8:31-39
Jeremiah 17:7-8

In moments of self-inadequacy, when we struggle with God's timeline or our future plans, our confidence can be shaken. These scriptures today emphasize that God is for us and not against us. We do not have to be afraid. His power is limitless; He can turn an impossible situation around in an instant. He is the creator of all things, and He is on our side. What a blessing! Another scripture states that He prepares a table for me in the presence of my enemies (Psalms 23:5). This means I can be surrounded by people who hate me and want to destroy me, but God's hand of protection is over me. God is helping you overcome the most difficult situations when it feels like everything is against you. He is making a way in the wilderness and rivers in the desert (Isaiah 43:19).

One thing I think about frequently is how certain I am that God has saved me from many destructive situations I don't even know about. I am confident in God's protection because I am His child. Scripture says that the Lord covers the righteous with His favor as a shield (Psalm 5:12). We don't know all of His plans, but I am confident that God is for me and that I have favor with God and man (Proverbs 3:4). There are places you can go and promotions you can receive because of your obedience and faithfulness to God. He will never leave you in a mess you have made for yourself; He will reach into the pit where you are and place your feet upon solid ground. If He did it for me, He can and will do it for you. Thank you, Jesus!

Reflect:

In what area of your life do you need to put your confidence in Christ? Ask Him to help you through that difficult situation today. Surrender it at His feet.

Pray:

Lord, thank You for the confidence I have in You. Help me to rest in the truth that You are for me and that nothing can separate me from Your love. When doubts or fears arise, remind me of Your promises that are yes and amen. I trust that in You, I am more than a conqueror. In Jesus' name, Amen.

LIVING AS A WOMAN
DAY 18

Proverbs 31:10-31

As a child of God and a wife, I know exactly who God has called me to be. Proverbs 31 is packed with godly wisdom for women to read, whether you are single or in a relationship. When I read it, I am reminded there is always room for improvement. We know nobody is perfect—except one. This chapter is who I strive to become daily with the help of Jesus.

This is a journey of refinement. Like gold refined in the fire, I think of the melting process. Gold is refined in the fire to bring impurities to the surface so they can be removed. That is my prayer for you. Change doesn't happen overnight. This chapter encourages us women to be strong, work willingly for our husbands, and trust in the Lord at all times. This woman is clothed with strength and dignity; she laughs without fear of the future and has a heart to serve. She speaks wisely and with kindness and loving instruction is on her lips. She is not afraid of difficult circumstances, because she is confident that God is her source, not this world or economy. Lastly, her husband praises her, and her children call her blessed. I want to be more like this woman.

She does not self-sabotage situations or use others, but instead gives every difficulty to God and asks to be led by His Spirit. She keeps in step with the Spirit and is obedient, not making big or small decisions without first seeking the Lord. She doesn't gossip or speak poorly about others, but instead speaks kindly and does not compare herself to those around her. She is known at her church for being filled with faith and compassion, laying hands on others and praying for anyone in need at any time. She is a woman who is confident God will do everything He promises. She knows in her heart, without a shadow of a doubt, that God is working all things out for her good and the good of her family.

As women, we have all at one point in our lives tried to keep up with trends of this world and sometimes convinced ourselves we needed a little makeup or jewelry before leaving the house. But this next scripture is humbling and serves as a great reminder that the Lord looks at our hearts, not our outward appearance. 1 Peter 3:3 states that our adornment should be found in our hearts, with a quiet and gentle spirit, rather than in looks that will fade and perish. As children of God, we need to be presentable, as we are temples of the Holy Spirit and represent Christ. However, as we read today, there are many things much more important to the Lord than our looks. It's about the legacy we leave behind and the work we fulfill on earth to advance the kingdom. 1 Samuel 16:7 states, "For the Lord sees not as man sees: man looks on the outward appearance, but the Lord looks on the heart." The Lord cares more about what flows from our hearts and our heart posture, rather than the newest clothes or trends.

Reflect:

After reading Proverbs 31, choose one scripture within this chapter that you want to work on, and ask for guidance from the Holy Spirit. Write this down somewhere you will see it to read each day this week.

Pray:

Lord, I come before You desiring to grow into the woman You have called me to be—a woman of strength, virtue, and wisdom, as described in scripture today. Create in me a heart to serve others without grumbling or complaining. Show me how to be diligent and hardworking, and how to care for my family and others in a holy way. In Jesus' name, Amen.

JEHOVAH-RAPHA
DAY 19

Isaiah 53:5
1 Peter 2:24

Jehovah-Rapha is a Hebrew name for God that means "the Lord who heals". It is a name for God that appears in Exodus 15:26 where God declares, "I am the Lord who heals you". There are many stories in the New Testament about Jesus' work healing the sick during His time on earth. Because God never changes and is faithful throughout the ages, He still performs miracles, signs, and wonders today. One question I frequently hear is, "Why does God let bad things happen to good people?" This question leads us back to the fall of man when sin entered the world. When Eve convinced Adam to eat from the tree of the knowledge of good and evil, they both disobeyed God, allowing the enemy's lies to overtake them.

Since then, sin has separated everyone on earth from God. This is why God sent His one and only Son to die on the cross for all of mankind. When Jesus died for our sins, the veil was torn (Matthew 27:50-51). This signified that the old covenant was done away with, and the new covenant established by Christ's blood provided a perfect and complete atonement for sin. People would no longer need to sacrifice an animal free of blemish to temporarily cover their sins. God removed the separation between Himself and humanity, granting us divine access to a relationship with Him. In doing so, Jesus paid the ultimate price.

When He paid the ultimate price, scripture says that by His stripes (or beatings) we are healed (Isaiah 53:5). We received not only forgiveness for our sins but also healing from sickness and disease in our bodies. Jesus' suffering extends beyond spiritual restoration to include healing for our physical bodies.

During my husband's illness this past year, we put up healing scriptures on many sticky notes throughout our house. They were on every door and scattered randomly. We read them every time we saw them and thanked God for His healing. One of my favorites is, "The Lord sustains him on their sickbed; in his illness you restore him to full health" (Psalm 41:3). God has healed my husband multiple times, performing miracles that no human mind could comprehend. On one occasion, the physician had no idea how my husband was completely healed. It made no scientific sense. I will testify and proclaim that God still performs miracles! If he did it back then, He will do it again.

When you begin to believe that God can and will heal you and your body, it becomes a reality. When God's Word becomes real to you, your faith allows you to access your healing. You have to take ahold of this promise. How can Jesus heal you if you don't believe that He is your healer? Sometimes healing may take time, but at other times, it can be immediate or sudden.

We must believe God's Word and have faith that His promises are true to access all that God has for us. There are so many scriptures in the Bible recounting how Jesus healed the sick and raised the dead when He walked the earth. The best part is that God is the same yesterday, today, and forever. Take God at His word and receive your healing today. Healing is not only for sickness and disease but for every heartache and broken situation.

Reflect:

How does the name Jehovah-Rapha, "The Lord who heals," deepen your understanding of God's character? How can you cultivate patience and trust in God when healing doesn't come immediately?

Pray:

Lord, I come before You seeking Your healing touch. Thank You, God, for the healing virtue that flows through my body daily. I thank You for the precious blood of Jesus. Thank You, Lord, that You are my healer and that You can do all things. May Your peace and strength surround me as I trust in Your perfect care. In Jesus' name, Amen.

GETTING OUT OF THE WAY
DAY 20

Exodus 3:1-15
Exodus 4:1-14
2 Corinthians 3:5

There are many lessons to be learned in these two chapters. If you know the story of Moses, you can recall that God asked him to bring the people of Israel out of Egypt. And let's be honest, that's a big ask. However, even in our own lives, God gives us tasks that seem impossible to our natural mind. Although God told Moses exactly what to do and exactly what to say, Moses continued to offer up excuses as for why he wasn't the man fit for the job. If you are anything like me, you sometimes do the same thing. We often don't feel qualified, good enough, or worthy enough to do what God asks of us. This is similar to how I reacted when God told me to write this book.

But after all the excuses Moses gave to God, He didn't just say "never mind" and give up on him. But, because of God's goodness and faithfulness, He met Moses where he was and offered to send Aaron to help him and speak for him. Remember, God never left their side and helped them every step of the way. I want to reassure you that God will never leave you nor forsake you. He is waiting for your "yes" to bring you through the Red Sea to the other side where your victory lies as you watch your enemies drown. Whatever God has placed on your heart to do, give Him your "yes." Give Him your "yes" today, because, as the Bible depicts today, doing what the Lord asks you to do affects more than just you, but others around you. There is someone waiting for your yes. When you say yes to God, everything else falls into place. If He told you to do it, He will bring you through it. The battle is already won in Jesus' name!

God sees your potential. He is waiting for your "yes"! If God is for us, who can be against us? He has qualified you to go forth and fulfill the word He has given you. Stop second-guessing God!

Reflect:

What has God asked or called you to do that you are questioning or second-guessing? What are you delaying that God has asked you to do NOW? It's time to get started!

Pray:

Lord, thank You for calling me to walk closely with You. Help me to surrender my own plans, trusting that Your way is higher, and Your timing is perfect. Give me the courage to say yes to You, even when situations look difficult, uncertain, or impossible. Grant me strength to obey where You lead me in every step I take, big or small. In Jesus' name, Amen.

THE ROOT OF BITTERNESS
DAY 21

John 8:1-11
Luke 6:37

Sometimes, it can be trying to forgive people who have caused pain in our lives. Often, we say we have "forgiven" someone, but we still hold onto what happened in the back of our minds or hold it over their heads. We quickly claim to "forgive" that person, but then we harbor a grudge for the rest of our lives. However, let's remember that God forgives us when we repent with a sincere and humble heart. One of my favorite scriptures reads, "He does not deal with us according to our sins and does not repay us according to our iniquities" (Psalm 103:10).

God is so compassionate; He is quick to forgive us when we sincerely repent. I'll never forget when Peter came up to Jesus in Matthew 18:21-22 asking, "Lord, how often will my brother sin against me, and I forgive him? As many as seven times?" And Jesus said to him, "I do not say to you seven times, but seventy-seven times." Let's be real, I don't keep count of all the times someone has hurt me or done me wrong. But we are called to forgive others as many times as it takes. And yes, that also means forgiving someone without ever receiving an apology. Let it go.

Most people don't realize when we fail to forgive others and hold grudges, we are letting a situation continue to hurt us. We also allow bitterness to manifest and grow in our lives, damaging our hearts. Don't waste your days living in self-pity. Aren't we called to love our enemies and be kind to one another? How can we expect to resemble Jesus when we still hold a grudge from a past hurt seven or ten years ago? If God is love and love keeps no record of wrongs, why do we carry grudges around like a box of rocks? Over time, those rocks get heavier and heavier.

In John 8, a woman was brought to Jesus who had committed adultery, and the law commanded that she be stoned to death. The first thing Jesus said to everyone was, "Let him who is without sin among you be the first to throw a stone at her." Then, one by one, everyone walked away. The moral of this story for today's devotional is to drop every stone of hurt and offense and refrain from throwing them back at others who have wronged us. Instead, we need to look in the mirror and recognize that we are not perfect; there are many things we have done wrong in our lives and people we have hurt along the way. We must walk in love even when it's hard. We have all fallen short at times, but we are justified by His grace through the redemption of Jesus Christ (Romans 3:23-24). Scripture reads that "hatred stirs up strife, but love covers all offenses." (Proverbs 10:12).

Jesus says in Matthew 6:14, "For if you forgive others their trespasses, your heavenly Father will also forgive you." A great way to start forgiving people in your heart is to pray for them until you genuinely forgive them. Let God handle the rest; He will mend our broken hearts and bind up our wounds (Psalm 147:3).

Reflect:

Who is God leading you to forgive in your life today? What grudges do you need to let go of?

Pray:

Lord, I ask you to uproot any unforgiveness or bitterness in my heart today and replace it with Your perfect love and kindness. Help me be an imitator of you today and every day, and love others without keeping a record of wrongs. Teach me to let go of resentment and anger and let me forgive not only with my words but with my heart. In Jesus' name, Amen.

YOUR CIRCLE MATTERS
DAY 22

Luke 5:17-26

Having close, Christian friends has been monumental in my life. In this scripture, a paralyzed man's four friends brought him up to the roof to get him closer to Jesus for healing. Talk about faith. I mean they climbed the actual roof and then tore it off! One thing to pay attention to here is verse 20. Scripture says, "And when he saw their faith," meaning Jesus not only perceived the paralyzed man's faith but also glimpsed the faith of each of his friends. Each of them knew that if they could just get to Jesus, the paralyzed man would be healed. That is so powerful. This scripture goes to show who you hang around matters! If you surround yourself with people who are full of faith, you will watch your own faith grow. Scripture also says in 1 Corinthians 15:33 that, "bad company ruins good morals". We have to be cautious of who we hang around.

Sometimes, friendships can be difficult and cause pain. If you haven't found out yet, people will let you down in this lifetime. But I have good news: there is a friend who sticks closer than a brother...and it's Jesus (Proverbs 18:24). He is the perfect friend and will never let us down. I challenge you to start going to Jesus first before your friends. When you are hurt, have the messy, tearful, and hard conversations with Him first, because He can provide peace and comfort like no other earthly friend can. Most times, through prayer, God takes care of any worries, stress, and past hurts from friendships.

Another amazing thing about Jesus is that He makes all things new. God is a creator. He has the ability to restore everything and anything. I'm not only talking about restoring our heartbreaks and removing all pain, suffering, and trauma caused by previous relationships, but also about restoring our friendships like never before. He also will draw new meaningful friends into our lives if we ask Him.

Finding and sticking with faith-filled friends is essential to our faith walk. We need friends who will encourage us to pray about difficult situations and go to battle in prayer for us and our circumstances. The most important aspect of having godly friendships is that they draw us closer to Jesus. My circle of friends encourage me to grow deeper in my relationship with the Lord and stand in belief with me. They push me to rely on God and remind me of His promises and comfort in moments of doubt. Proverbs 27:17 states, "Iron sharpens iron, and one man sharpens another." Good friends encourage us to remain rooted in Christ.

God designed us to live in community and in harmony with one another. Each friendship I have bears fruit in my life, and I have people who stand alongside me in times of need. I am so thankful for the love and support they offer. I encourage you to reflect on your friendships today. Which friends are not bringing you closer to Christ? Who do you want to spend more time with? As you have probably heard a time or two, you eventually become who you hang around.

Reflect:

Will your friends tear off the roof to bring you closer to Jesus, or are your friends drawing you away from the Lord? Take this time to reflect on the friendships closest to you.

Pray:

Lord, thank You for the gift of friendship and for the blessing of sharing life with others who love and follow You. I pray for friendships that are deeply rooted in Your truth, strengthened by love, and centered around Jesus. Bring people into my life who will encourage me in my faith, challenge me to grow, and walk with me in both joy and struggle. Lord, protect the friendships that honor You and draw me nearer to You. May I be a faithful friend who reflects Your love and kindness in return. In Jesus' name, Amen.

LIVING CONTENTLY
DAY 23

Hebrews 13:5
Psalm 23:1-6

Every time I read the New Testament, scriptures about contentment always stand out to me. In today's world, flooded with influencers having the best and biggest things showcased on social media, it can be extremely hard to be content with what we have if we are always wanting more. Before I cut back on my social media usage, I constantly compared myself to others. Comparison will force you to feel like you are behind in life, lagging behind all of your friends your age who are hitting major life milestones. Comparison is the thief of all joy.

In Luke 12:15 scripture reads, "Take care, and be on your guard against all covetousness, for one's life does not consist in the abundance of his possessions." Before you find yourself in a place of want, wanting the most stylish clothes or the best house out of all your friends, read that again. Matthew 6:19 also tells us not to lay up our treasures on this earth, but in heaven. News flash: this world will pass away with everything in it. We can't take any of the possessions we own on earth into heaven, not even the money sitting in our bank accounts. But I can assure you that God's Word will never pass away (Isaiah 40:8). Only Jesus can fill an empty void, not an abundance of possessions or money.

With this in mind, let's not forget to be thankful for all the things we are blessed to have. In 1 Timothy 6:6-8 Paul writes, "Godliness with contentment is great gain, for we brought nothing into the world, and we cannot take anything out of the world. But if we have food and clothing, with these we will be content." Gratitude is a declaration of our faith, resting in the truth that God is good no matter what, awakening our hearts to His unchanging character.

Wow. How often do we forget to thank God for meeting our most basic needs? Psalm 23 starts by saying, "the Lord is my shepherd; I shall not want." As a child of God, He alone is my provider. God ensures I have more than enough and gives me everything I have to enjoy. Take a moment today to thank God and praise Him for the food in your pantry or fridge and the roof over your head. Jesus will always make sure we have what we need to fulfill the purpose He has set for our lives. Let's stop craving more earthly treasures and start thanking our heavenly Father for our eternal inheritance. Set your mind on things above, not on things of this world. We are told to seek first the kingdom of God, and all of these things will be added to us (Matthew 6:33).

Reflect:

Is God enough for you? Are you content with what you have, or are you constantly finding yourself wanting more? How can you move from a place of want to a place of contentment today?

Pray:

Lord, thank You for all You have given me. Help me find contentment in every season, knowing that You are my provider and that Your grace is enough. Teach me to trust that I have all I need in You and to let go of any longing that distracts me from Your goodness. Fill my heart with gratitude, and help me to live simply and joyfully, finding peace in Your presence. May my life reflect satisfaction and trust in Your perfect plan. In Jesus' name, Amen.

HARDSHIP AS A CHRISTIAN
DAY 24

James 1:2-4
1 Peter 4:12-19
2 Corinthians 4:8-10

Nobody said life would be easy. Grief, pain, and disappointment are all difficult roads to travel. Contrary to what some might think, as Christians, we will still face struggles and trials. In today's scripture, we are encouraged to "count it all joy when we face trials of various kinds." James knew that God could use even the most challenging situations to build in us faith that endures and trust in Him that is unshakable. When we surrender our pain to Him, we encounter a God who is present in our suffering, who understands our pain, and who helps us walk through it. In Hebrews we read, "For we do not have a high priest who is unable to sympathize with our weaknesses, but one who in every respect has been tempted as we are, yet without sin" (Hebrews 4:15). Jesus understands what it is like to be human. He has experienced every single emotion we have. How comforting is that?

When we look to Jesus, we find the ultimate example of suffering with purpose. His life on earth was filled with hardship, rejection, and pain, yet He endured it all with love and humility. He willingly laid down His life for us. There is no greater love than this (John 15:13). In His greatest and painful sacrifice, He knew there was a greater purpose for His suffering.

When we feel beaten down and broken, God gives us beauty for ashes. He can make a broken situation beautiful once again. We aren't meant to carry heavy burdens and pain all on our own. Matthew 11:30 reassures us that His yoke is easy, and His burden is light. Jesus offers us rest when we bring our most difficult situations and heartbreak to Him.

Today, if you are facing a season of suffering, remember that God sees you and he will restore you. John 16:33 reads, "In this world you will have tribulation. But take heart; I have overcome the world." Christ knew we would have struggles when sin entered the world, but He offers us living hope. When our hope rests solely in the King of Kings, we experience a comfort that cannot be taken away by any heartache.

Today, lean into His presence, allow Him to strengthen you, and hold fast to the truth that He is actively working in you and transforming you—even through the hardest of times. After we have suffered a little while, God will restore, confirm, strengthen, and establish us (1 Peter 5:10).

Reflect:

In what ways can you see God moving in your current circumstances? How might He be refining or shaping you in this season of hardship? What is He teaching you today?

Pray:

Lord, thank You for being with me in my suffering. I fix my eyes on You today, regardless of my circumstances. I thank you for using the hardest moments to shape me, prepare me, and draw me closer to You. Give me strength to persevere and faith to trust in Your purpose. In Jesus' name, Amen.

REJOICING THROUGH LIFE
DAY 25

Psalm 118:24
Matthew 12:33

Life is a gift from God. His breath is in our lungs at this very moment. When God created us in our mother's womb, the Bible says God knew us by name before we were born (Jeremiah 1:5). God is the reason we are all breathing and alive right now. There are many scriptures in the Bible that tell us we were created to praise and worship our Heavenly Father (Psalm 29:1-2, Ephesians 1:3-6, 1 Corinthians 10:31).

How can we worship God and be thankful for everything He has blessed us with when we walk through life with a frown on our faces, moping around all day, mad at the world or at one another? One thing the Holy Spirit revealed to me was this: How will non-believers tell us apart? How will others know that God lives inside us if we act like everyone else in this world? One way,

I believe, is by the joy in my heart, from which all things flow. I will not be led by my emotions and the ups and downs of my feelings, but I will be led by truth.

The Word today says we will be able to tell a difference by their "fruits," which are the fruit of the Spirit. No good tree can bear bad fruit, and no bad tree good fruit. The fruit of the spirit includes love, joy, peace, patience, kindness, goodness, faithfulness, gentleness, and self-control (Galatians 5:22-23). Let me let you in on a little secret: One reason people can tell me apart is because I have JOY. I walk around joyful every day, with a smile on my face. People have even asked me before, "What are you always so happy about?" One simple answer: Jesus. He has turned my mourning into joy! Plus, it's a great conversation starter.

As I mentioned earlier, I make it a point to spend time in God's presence before I start each day. Psalm 16:11 reads, "You make known to me the path of life; in your presence there is fullness of joy; at your right hand are pleasures forevermore." I'm telling you, spending time with the Lord before you start your day can shift your mood and change the outcome of your entire day. Try it and see what happens!

Many people get joy and happiness confused; they are not interchangeable. Joy is not happiness. Happiness is a feeling. Joy is a choice. Happiness is fleeting, coming and going based on our circumstances. Joy is constant and does not depend on our circumstances.

I know all of us have said at one point in our lives, "It feels like I just can't catch a break." Girl, me too. As I wrote yesterday, in this life we will have trials and difficulties. But this is the day the Lord has made; I will rejoice and be glad in it! Each day is filled with God opportunities, arranged by God alone, that await us.

As I said earlier about peace, I'm not letting any circumstance steal my joy. Because the Holy Spirit resides in me, joy resides in me as well. Choose joy today no matter what life throws at you. Sometimes we just need to look up, open our eyes, and thank God for the things right in front of us. We have so much in life to be thankful for.

Reflect:

In what area of your life do you need to do more rejoicing? How can you cultivate joy today despite your circumstances?

Pray:

Father, thank You for this day You have created, filled with new God opportunities that await me. Fill my heart with gladness and a spirit of worship, so that I may praise You with all that I am. Help me to worship You wholeheartedly, regardless of my circumstances, knowing that true joy is found in You alone. In Jesus' name, Amen.

FREEDOM IN CHRIST
DAY 26

2 Corinthians 3:17
Galatians 5:1

I am so thankful for growth. I remember when I was in high school and college, I cared so much about what people thought of me. One person's negative comment could ruin my day because I would let it live in the back of my mind. What a waste of a day! Today, I only care about one opinion: what God thinks of me. This revelation helped me move away from being a people-pleaser.

With some practice and the help of the Holy Spirit, I am able to let every hurtful situation or unkind word spoken roll right off my back. In reality, I would rather please God and let many people down instead of pleasing others while letting God down. Scripture says, "For the gate is narrow and the way is hard that leads to life, and those who find it are few" (Matthew 7:14). Jesus tells us that the wide gate is the path that leads to destruction, which many will take. But the path to eternal life is narrow, and it is a life that is laid down and yielded to Christ, living according to His will.

Throughout Jesus' time on earth, we read that He was never a people-pleaser, but a Father-pleaser. When we say we want to look more like Jesus, we must let go of living up to the world's standards and caring so heavily about what others think of us. I'm no longer seeking applause or recognition from others. Our lives on earth should point others to Christ. If they don't, we need to re-evaluate how we are living and who we are living for. Are we living for ourselves and our selfish ambitions, or are we living for Christ? When we are surrendered to Christ, the pressures of pleasing man quickly fade away. We will have to answer to only one—Jesus.

God also gives us freedom from sin. Scripture says we must consider ourselves dead to sin and alive in Christ Jesus! We are also free from oppression, depression, and any addiction that once had a grip on us. When we accept Jesus into our hearts and ask Him to come and change our lives, He makes all things new. Whom the Son sets free is free indeed (John 8:34-36). If the Spirit of God is leading me, then I am free from others' opinions and judgments. Today, I am fully free from the bondage of sin and other's opinions that once held me captive.

Reflect:

What does living surrendered to Christ look like for you in your day-to-day life? Are there areas where you are still holding onto old patterns or addictions that need to be surrendered to Christ?

Pray:

Lord, thank You for the freedom I have in Christ. Help me to live for Your approval alone and I release the need to please others. Teach me to follow Jesus' example of honoring You above all and to walk in freedom from sin. May my life point others to You, and may I find my identity in Christ alone. In Jesus' name, Amen.

OUR THOUGHT LIFE
DAY 27

Philippians 4:8-9
2 Corinthians 10:5

Scripture says we are to write the Word on the tablet of our hearts (Proverbs 3:3). When we read and meditate on God's Word day and night, we start to inscribe it on our hearts, and it then begins to produce good fruit within us. In our thought life, however, it is easy to allow small thoughts to creep in that do not align with God's Word. Today we read that the Word actually tells us exactly what to think about. Why, then, are we so quick to envision the worst possible outcome of a situation or flood our minds with negativity and "what ifs"?

We need to recognize a negative thought as soon as it arises and shut it down. This is what it means to take every thought captive and obey God. I will only allow pure and honorable thoughts into my mind. When God's Word is imprinted on our hearts and we can recite scripture in the back of our minds when a negative thought comes, we need to speak the Word out loud. It is almost impossible to fight thoughts with thoughts, but it is possible to fight thoughts with words—especially the living and active Word of God. Every word in the Bible is breathed out by God and is full of power and authority.

There is immense power in our words when they align with God's. The Bible says we can move mountains with our words. We are to speak to the mountain, and it shall be moved (Mark 11:23). The next time your thoughts do not align with God's Word, I encourage you to have scripture written down ready to confess over your life. Only truth may reside here; fear and anxiety cannot remain. Check your thoughts at the door!

Reflect:

What thoughts have you been allowing to dwell in your mind? Do these thoughts about yourself, others, or a situation align with God's Word? If not, how can you change?

Pray:

Lord, give me supernatural strength to take every thought captive and make it obedient to You. Guard my mind from negativity, worry, and lies, and fill my thoughts with Your truth, peace, and love. Teach me to focus on what is pure, lovely, and praiseworthy, and guide my heart to think in ways that honor You. In Jesus' name, Amen.

YOU MUST DECIDE
DAY 28

1 John 2:15-17
James 4:4-8
Romans 12:2

There are many Christians living half in and half out of the world and all it has to offer. These people are lukewarm, aware that there is a God but not completely living for Him. These scriptures clearly state you are either a friend of God or a friend of the world. If you are a friend of the world, you are an enemy of God. That is a frightening thought, as the standards of this world and the pride of life do not align with Christ's will for our lives; they are directly opposite of His character.

To love the world is to be a part of it, following the crowd and doing what everyone else is doing, such as listening to secular music and watching horror films. I don't know about you, but I am giving no foothold or opportunity to Satan in my house. Everything you are doing that does not bring glory to God is cracking a door open for the enemy to enter. No wonder why we have an unsettling feeling while watching inappropriate movies or are overtaken with fear after we watch a horror film. For me, conviction sets in when I know I shouldn't be watching or listening to something. Scripture emphasizes the importance of guarding your mind and heart (Proverbs 4:23).

We are called to be set apart from this world and to live different. As Trya Rains wrote in her book "Virtue: Living Uncommon in a Common World", we are to swim against the common current. We live in this world, but we are not of this world. This means we must not compromise our values and behaviors to conform to those around us. Christ says not to love this world, because it will pass away along with every evil thing in it. So as for me and my house, we will serve the Lord (Joshua 24:15).

Our flesh is not saved, but our soul is. Our flesh and spirit are constantly at war with each other, which is why we must discipline our bodies. Our flesh should submit to our spirit. We must exercise self-control and discipline ourselves to walk in holiness, not compromising God's Word to fit our "lifestyle." If you believe the Word and want to live by it, you cannot pick and choose which scriptures to apply to your life; you must obey all of it.

In 1 Corinthians 9:24-27, Paul states that he disciplines his body and keeps it under control because our flesh desires things contrary to the spirit (Galatians 5:17). Our flesh wants to live like this world and partake in what feels good. However, like Paul, we must exercise self-control and starve our flesh. We must remain rooted in righteousness and read God's Word daily to feed our spirit so it may be stronger than our flesh. Fasting and prayer are essential to do this.

Scripture also says that God yearns jealously over the spirit He has made to dwell in us (James 4:5). He wants our time, attention, fellowship, and our heart. He longs for us to remain close to Him, avoiding sin that pulls us away. I encourage you to let your manner of life be worthy of the gospel of Christ, walking in a manner pleasing to the Lord and not to man. We are told today not to conform to the patterns of this world. Living like those in the world and loving the world both come at a great cost.

Reflect:

In what ways does your life reflect the values of God's kingdom? Do you find yourself struggling with compromising your faith in certain areas to fit in with the crowd? What specific steps can you take to be more fully committed to God?

Pray:

Lord, help me to live fully for You, not compromising with the world or seeking its approval. Strengthen my spirit to resist the desires of the flesh and walk in holiness. Teach me to discipline my body and align my life with Your Word for the kingdom. Draw me closer to You, Lord, and help me live a life worthy of the gospel. In Jesus' name, Amen.

THE GREAT COMMISSION
DAY 29

Mark 16:14-20

As believers of Jesus Christ, we are called to "go into all the world and proclaim the gospel to the whole creation." I believe God calls some people to the five-fold ministry, but I am not one of them. However, I am still called to go into my world and preach the gospel. I may not be a missionary or a pastor, but there are people in my life whom I can reach—my boss, my co-workers, my friends, and friends of friends whom I encounter daily. These are the people in my circle I can shower with the love of Christ and witness to.

I am a firm believer that God has strategically placed me exactly where I am for a reason. God is intentional. He placed me at my job to reach the lost in my community. He placed me in my church to comfort and serve others. Even when it doesn't look or seem like

He is working, He is arranging all the puzzle pieces to fit together seamlessly, all for His glory and to make Him known. He has done the same for you. He is not done writing your story.

One scripture that will stick with me forever is, "How are they to believe in Him of whom they have never heard" (Romans 10:14)? There are people out there who are searching for truth. How can we plant the seeds of Christ in others' hearts if we never tell them about Jesus?

I learned that it is not our job to save souls—only Christ can do that heavy lifting—but we are called to sow the seeds of the gospel and to love others like Jesus does. I'm not sure if you've ever experienced a pull on your spirit to talk to someone about Jesus, but I have. I am sure of this: never ignore the leading of the Holy Spirit. You might be the confirmation that someone needs to give their life to Christ. You might be the only person whom Jesus leads to pray for that individual. Maybe someone in your community or neighborhood has been waiting for you to share your testimony and tell them about Jesus.

It can be nerve-racking talking to someone about Jesus, but God has equipped you with everything you need to share His message. I pray a new boldness rises up within your spirit. Satan doesn't want you to tell anyone about Jesus because he wants to bring as many souls with him to hell when Jesus returns. My prayer before I minister to people is that the Holy Spirit speaks through me when I open my mouth, so it is not I who speaks, but Christ through me (Matthew 10:20). God knows exactly what that person needs to hear; I am the willing vessel He uses to reach their heart.

If you know that God sent His one and only Son to die for our sins, rose on the third day, and is now seated in heaven with Christ, you can go preach the good news to everyone. Sharing your testimony about how God saved you and changed your life can be moving to others. It just takes one conversation about Christ, then God will intentionally reveal Himself to them in a way they can understand. If people are not open or willing to receive your words, Matthew 10:14 says, "Shake off the dust from your feet when you leave that house or town." Move on to reach the next person, because there are many who are lost and hungry for truth, even if they don't realize it yet.

In the words of Pastor Joel Sims, "God can't save the soul if you don't sow the seed". How beautiful are the feet of those who preach the good news (Romans 10:15). God will reward your obedience. Be willing to step out in faith today!

Reflect:

Who in your life is God calling you to share the gospel with? How can you be more intentional about sharing your faith in your everyday environments? I challenge you to obey the Holy Spirit and see what He can do.

Pray:

Lord, thank You for the greatest calling—to share the good news of Jesus with those around me. Help me to be bold and obedient, trusting that You will speak through me as I step out in faith. Give me the courage to speak the truth, even when it feels intimidating, and help me to always listen to the Holy Spirit's prompting. Use my testimony to point others to You and give me the wisdom to know when to speak and when to listen. In Jesus' name, Amen.

VESSELS FOR CHRIST
DAY 30

2 Timothy 2:20-26

As Christians, we are designed by God and for God. We are meant to be used as vessels. This scripture explains two types of vessels: one for honorable use and one for dishonorable use. Surely, we all want to be a vessel of honorable use for the Lord. When the Lord gives me an assignment, I want to fulfill it quickly without hesitation. If the Lord trusts us with little, then He will trust us with much (Luke 16:10). There is a quote by Mark Hankins that says, "We get some places because we trust God, but we get other places because God trusts us". Can God trust you to answer His call and obey him without hesitation?

To be used as a vessel for honorable use, we must be obedient to the Lord. We must also flee from sin and renew ourselves in the Word of God. When we renew our minds with the Word, we begin to look more like Jesus as we seek Him. Vessels for honorable use are those who pursue things that reflect God's character and avoid sinful desires and ways of the wicked. Being a vessel means giving God your "yes" and being a servant of God, taking up your cross to follow Him. Instead of engaging in arguments, we are called to respond with kindness, patience, and a readiness to teach the truth. It is important to live a life of humility and integrity, focusing on honoring and pleasing the Lord in all we speak and pursue.

Reflect:

How can you be a vessel of honorable use for the Lord today? How can you pursue holiness in your everyday life, especially in your relationships and actions?

Pray:

Lord, help me to live a life of obedience, purity, and integrity, reflecting Your character in all I do. Teach me to respond with kindness, patience, and gentleness, serving You with a humble heart. Use me as a vessel for honorable use and guide me to fulfill the calling You've placed on my life. May my obedience bring honor and glory to Your name. In Jesus' name, Amen.

LIVING WATER
DAY 31

John 4:13-15

Water is essential to our everyday life. Every cell, organ, and function in our body needs water to survive. In today's scripture, Jesus speaks about a new thirst and a different kind of water. A living water. In our busy lives, we can easily seek fulfillment from sources that promise temporary satisfaction but leave us empty and yearning for more. Jesus has come so we can have life and have it abundantly (John 10:10). He invites us to come to Him, allowing Him to fill, restore, and transform us. When we are filled, we begin to pour out to those around us who are thirsty and need a Savior.

In His conversation with the Samaritan woman, Jesus invited her to leave behind the things that never truly satisfied. He offered her "living water," the source of true refreshment, and an invitation to a relationship with God himself. Nothing else can satisfy us in this world. We were created to spend eternity with Christ. Our heart yearns for Jesus. As women, we too can experience this living water that brings life to our souls, heals our brokenness, quenches our deepest longings, and refreshes our spirit in ways nothing else can.

As Jesus begins to fill us and we come to know Him on a deeper level, we will continue to hunger and thirst for righteousness. That's when our mindset begins to shift—more of Him and less of me. He must increase; I must decrease (John 3:30). This is what it means to lay down our lives and live for Christ alone. It is no longer I who live, but Christ who lives in me (Galatians 2:20). People will continue to search this earth for that one thing until they hear about and encounter Jesus. Only Christ alone will satisfy.

Reflect:

In what areas of your life do you feel challenged to surrender fully to Christ? Who are the people in your life who might be thirsty for this living water?

Pray:

Thank You God for offering me living water that satisfies my deepest thirst. Fill me with Your presence and refresh my soul, so that I can pour out Your love to those around me. Teach me to hunger and thirst for righteousness and to live for You alone. In Jesus' name, Amen.

GOD WANTS YOUR HEART

If you read this book and aren't sure where you stand with the Lord, I encourage you to keep reading this page.

Salvation is the gift of God's grace, extended to each of us through the death and resurrection of Jesus Christ. To be "saved" means to accept this gift, receive Jesus as Lord, and enter into a relationship with God. It is more than just saying words; it's about a deep transformation that begins with our heart.

God's love for us is so great that He sent His only Son, Jesus, to die on the cross for our sins. Romans 5:8 tells us, "But God shows His love for us in that while we were still sinners, Christ died for us." Jesus took on our sins, bearing our punishment so that we could be forgiven and reconciled to God. Through His resurrection, Jesus conquered sin and death, giving us the promise of eternal life with Christ.

Salvation is God's gift to us (Ephesians 2:8-9). We don't earn it by being "good enough" or through good works. When we recognize our need for Him and turn to Him in faith, confessing our sins and believing that Jesus is Lord, He has mercy on us. Jesus is not a puppet master; He left this decision up to us. When we accept Christ into our heart, we begin a new journey with Christ, one where we are forgiven and redeemed by His blood. We then begin to change from the inside out if we desire to live for Christ. If you're ready to accept this gift, you can pray this prayer below. In the Bible, there is no true prayer of salvation, but we are told to confess with our mouth that Jesus is Lord of our lives and believe in our hearts that God raised Christ from the dead (Romans 10:9). God promises to meet you in this moment and begin a new work in you as you build a relationship with Him.

Pray:

Lord, I come before You knowing that I am a sinner in need of Your grace. I believe that Jesus is Your Son, that He died for my sins, and that He rose from the dead. Today, I choose to turn from my sins and invite Jesus into my heart as my Savior and Lord. Help me to walk with You every day, growing in faith and reflecting Your love. Thank You for this new beginning.

In Jesus' name,
Amen.

A NOTE FROM THE AUTHOR

Thank you for taking the time to journey through these pages. When God placed it upon my heart to write a book last year, I was confident He had a beautiful plan to touch the hearts of women He intended to reach.

Writing this book has been a testament to God's goodness and faithfulness, and all the glory belongs to Him alone. True devotion begins by cultivating the daily discipline of immersing yourself in His Word. I hope throughout this book, you've seen how His presence can bring transformation, joy, and new meaning to your life. I pray you will never be the same.

Remember, you are never alone. The Lord is the fourth man in the fire with you. You are loved by Him and called to a life of abundance in Christ. When you seek Him with your whole heart, there you will find Him. May this book serve as a reminder that God's plan for you is far greater than anything you could ever imagine.

Thank you for reading—it means more than words could ever express, and I am forever grateful.

With love and gratitude,

Alexandra

"Now to him who is able to do far more abundantly than all that we ask or think, according to the power at work within us, to him be the glory in the church and in Christ Jesus throughout all generations, forever and ever. Amen."

Ephesians 3:20-21 ESV